TAB A

1. Punch out circle and slit
2. Twist circle into a cone following the direction of the arrows till Tab A is to the right of Tab B
3. Fold Tab A to the outside and Tab B to the inside to secure the cup

TAB B

ADVENTURE INCLUDED

Not only is this book packed with information, it comes with several survival tools to keep you safe and sound in the wild.

THE BOOK
Use pages as fire tinder

REFLECTIVE SHEET
Signal an SOS or start a fire

FOLDABLE CUP
Collect emergency water

REFLECTIVE STICKERS
Mark your surroundings

STRING BINDING
Remove for extra string

Brimming with creative inspiration, how-to projects, and useful information to enrich your everyday life, Quarto Knows is a favorite destination for those pursuing their interests and passions. Visit our site and dig deeper with our books into your area of interest: Quarto Creates, Quarto Cooks, Quarto Homes, Quarto Lives, Quarto Drives, Quarto Explores, Quarto Gifts, or Quarto Kids.

19 20 21 22 23   6 5 4 3 2

ISBN: 978-1-6038-0409-7

Author: Marc Sumerak
Design: Andrew Hess
Editorial: Nancy Cortelyou
Production: Cindy Curren
Image research: Farley Bookout

Printed, manufactured, and assembled in China/ Singapore, 06/19.

MIX
Paper from
responsible sources
FSC® C017606

Disclaimer text: You should NEVER put yourself in dangerous situations to test whether the advice in this book really works. The publisher cannot accept responsibility for any injuries, damage, loss, or prosecutions resulting from the information in this book.

171066

SURVIVAL HANDBOOK

AN ESSENTIAL COMPANION TO THE GREAT OUTDOORS

MARC SUMERAK

CONTENTS

Watch for this symbol throughout the book! These information boxes let you know how to use the extras located at the front of the book.

INTRODUCTION

SURVIVAL ISN'T EASY.

No matter who you are or where you may be, each and every day is full of unique challenges that must be conquered if you hope to endure and thrive. As you grow, you learn the vital skills that will help you succeed in life and triumph over adversity. In some extreme situations, however, the essential skills required to survive don't come quite so naturally.

That's where this book comes in, to help teach you exactly what you need to know to make it through even the most unexpected and unforgiving circumstances. In these pages, you'll learn how to make a shelter, build a fire, locate clean water, forage for food, avoid deadly animals, protect yourself from bad weather, and find your way back home safely afterwards.

Whether you're lost in the wilderness or buried by an avalanche, knowing these essential emergency survival skills could literally mean the difference between life and death. They may not make the situation you're in any less frightening, but they will help to guarantee that you live to tell the tale.

You should NEVER put yourself in dangerous situations
to test whether the advice in this book really works.
The publisher cannot accept responsibility for any injuries, damage,
loss, or prosecutions resulting from the information in this book.

SURVIVAL BASICS

When you're planning a journey into the unknown, it's best to be prepared for any eventuality. Having the right equipment on hand (and knowing how to use it) can reduce almost any major disaster to a minor distraction. If you like to answer nature's beckoning call, you can at least be properly suited to survive!

9

WHAT TO PACK

TENT:
The simplest shelter solution, tents come in many easy-to-carry varieties. (See Pages 26–27.)

SLEEPING BAG:
A nice, cozy bedroll is a must for keeping warm on long, cold nights in the wild.

TARP:
A plastic tarp can be used to cover the ground in your tent or to create a makeshift shelter. A clear tarp can even be used to build a solar still. (See Page 62.)

RAIN GEAR:
A plastic poncho not only keeps your clothes dry, it can also be adapted for many of the same emergency uses as a tarp.

IN YOUR BACKPACK

WATER:

Start your trip with a few full water bottles, and be sure to have filters to purify emergency water sources. (See Pages 55–63.)

FOOD:

Bring enough food and snacks for your trip, plus a little extra, just in case. But be sure to properly store it so that you don't attract animals. (See Page 76.)

COOKING GEAR:

A durable pan will let you roast up anything you forage (see Pages 66–67), while a small pot will allow you to boil water (see Page 59). And don't forget a fork and knife!

TOOLS:

From simple scissors to the handy Swiss Army Knife (see Page 18), you'll need the proper tools to help you get the job done.

MORE TO PACK

ROPE:

Whether you need to secure a tent or build a snare, rope can be used for a variety of useful purposes—as long as you know how to tie a good knot. (See Pages 20-21.)

FIRE STARTERS:

If you want to build the perfect campfire (see Pages 46-49), you'll also need a way to light it. Make it easy on yourself and pack matches or other common fire-starting methods. (See Pages 50-51.)

FIRST AID KIT:

You never plan to get hurt, but be ready if you do with the proper bandages and medications. (See Pages 128-129.)

BUG SPRAY:

Many biting bugs can carry harmful diseases. (See Pages 96-99.) If you don't want your body to become their buffet, bring along a strong bug repellent.

SUN PROTECTION:

Prolonged sun exposure can be extremely harmful, so wear high-SPF sunscreen and bring sunglasses.

IN YOUR BACKPACK

BATTERIES:

Whether you bring a two-way radio (see Page 19) or a handheld GPS (see Page 115), you might need the prolonged power of a spare set of batteries.

EXTRA CLOTHING:

Temperatures and weather conditions can fluctuate in the wild, so always bring an extra set of warm, dry clothes. (See Page 16.)

MAP AND COMPASS:

Getting into the wilderness is easy. It's getting back out that can be tricky. Make sure you bring the proper tools to know where you're going. (See Pages 114–115.)

THIS BOOK:

What, you didn't think we'd expect you to memorize all of this, did you?

This book contains special features you won't want to be without: a reflective sheet to signal an SOS or start a fire; reflective stickers to mark your surroundings; a cup for emergency water collecting; and the string binding of this book if you need string. And don't forget the book's pages, which you can use as fire tinder.

HOW TO PACK

Every backpack is as different as the person who wears it. How *you* pack your gear is entirely up to you, but with all of the things that you need to bring, it's a good idea to keep them organized in a way that allows for easy access of the most important items. Here's a great example of how to pack your gear:

Light gear that you use often, like your map, compass, snacks, and rain poncho, should be packed at the top of the backpack.

Your **heaviest items**, like extra water, canned food, and cooking gear, should be kept in the upper-middle part of the pack, close to your back. This will also help you maintain your center of gravity.

The **mid-weight gear** used to set up camp, like your tent and tarp, as well as other small items you don't need to access regularly, can be packed in the lower-middle part of the pack.

Your **lightest gear**, like extra clothes, should be placed in the bottom section.

Your **sleeping bag** can be secured to the bottom of your backpack.

Any exterior pockets on the pack can be used for helpful **lightweight items**, like a flashlight, bug spray, or a small water bottle.

TRAIL TIP

Carrying a heavy backpack over long distances can be exhausting and potentially painful. Try to make sure your pack doesn't exceed twenty percent of your total body weight, if possible.

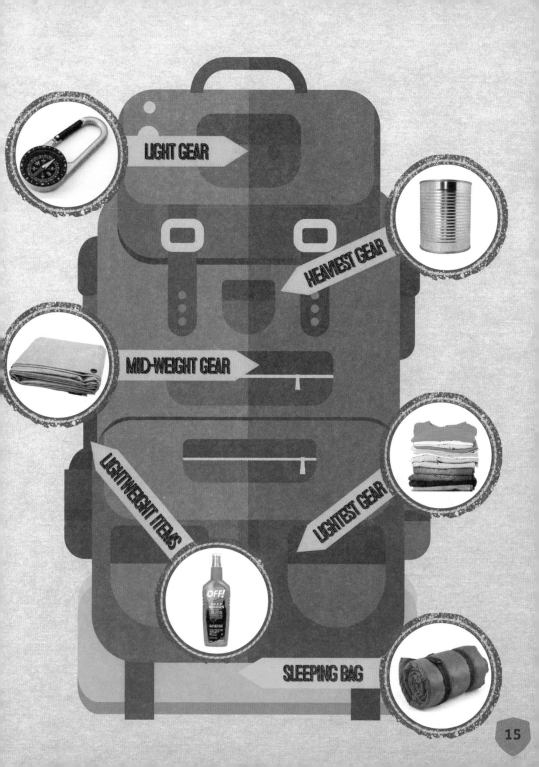

LIGHT GEAR

HEAVIEST GEAR

MID-WEIGHT GEAR

LIGHTWEIGHT ITEMS

LIGHTEST GEAR

SLEEPING BAG

WHAT TO WEAR

After you make sure you have the right gear for your adventure, it's time to make sure that you have the right clothing. Choosing your attire wisely can save you from getting soaked, sunburned, scraped, bitten, or covered in a rash. Here are some things to consider when picking out your ultimate camping outfit:

LAYERS:

Your pack already has more than enough in it, so if you're in a climate where the temperature and weather conditions vary, wearing multiple layers (which can be removed as needed) may be the most efficient way to go.

The **first layer** should be lightweight and easy to move in, made from a breathable fabric.

The **second layer** should be long and protective and made from something a bit more durable.

The **third layer** should be water- and wind-resistant, to protect you from the elements.

FIRST LAYER

SECOND LAYER

THIRD LAYER

FABRICS:

Synthetic materials like spandex are great at releasing moisture and excess heat, keeping you drier and cooler throughout the day. Natural fibers like cotton, although breathable, tend to trap moisture and can become quite uncomfortable under extreme conditions. An exception is wool—nature's wonder fabric.

DID YOU KNOW?

→ A wide-brimmed hat is great in all weather, protecting you from the rain and from sunburn.

→ A brightly colored scarf not only looks fashionable, but it can also be used as a signal in an emergency.

→ Survival isn't a fashion show. You should always choose function and comfort over style!

LENGTH:

While T-shirts and shorts may seem like the best answer in hot climates, long sleeves and pant legs can protect you from bug bites, sunburn, and contact with poisonous plants. If you're wearing a lightweight fabric, the additional length should provide extra safety without increasing the heat.

FOOTWEAR:

Sneakers and sandals aren't going to cut it in the wild. Make sure you have a good pair of waterproof hiking boots to help you traverse muddy trails and rugged terrain. Wool socks will keep you warm, dry, and protected, while still allowing your feet to breathe. Blister pads are helpful, too!

17

SURVIVAL

FLASHLIGHT:

A good fire provides a lot of light at night, but you can't take it with you when you need to leave your campsite. A strong flashlight is a must-have for navigating dark, unfamiliar terrain. A headlamp leaves your hands free to cook or make a fire or navigate your surroundings more easily.

SWISS ARMY KNIFE:

This popular multi-tool has tons of essential items packed into its tiny body, with most larger versions including a can opener, bottle opener, corkscrew, screwdrivers, file, and, of course, a selection of blades.

HATCHET:

A small handheld hatchet can be invaluable if you need to split firewood, chop down branches to build a shelter, or cut any other items that might be too thick for your knife.

TRAIL TIP

Knives and hatchets may look cool, but they also contribute to a large number of injuries in the wild. Always use great caution when wielding a bladed object.

TOOLS

SHOVEL:

Sure, you can dig with your hands, but a small hand shovel makes the job so much easier. Shovels can help you extinguish a fire, dig an emergency shelter, or even reach an underground water source.

BINOCULARS:

If you're not sure what awaits you off in the distance, binoculars can give you a better look without having to get up close and personal.

RADIO:

The wilderness may seem isolated, but a battery-powered radio can offer a small taste of the world back home. If you can get a signal, you'll have access to weather reports and some great tunes!

TWO-WAY RADIOS:

A different type of radio altogether, the two-way radio—also known as a walkie-talkie—is a great option when you're braving the wild with a friend, allowing you to keep in contact if you get separated.

KNOW YOUR
KNOTS

While you might tie knots every time you put on your shoes, it's important to know a variety of different knot styles, unless you want your shelter to collapse unexpectedly. There are hundreds of different ways to tie a knot, but the ones pictured here are some of the most useful and effective in a survival situation.

SQUARE KNOT:

This *joining* knot is a simple way to tie two ends of a rope together or to link two separate pieces of equally thick rope. It's useful for tying up a bundle, and is often used in first aid. It's called a square knot because it looks like it has four sides to it.

Step One:
Place the left strand over the right strand.

Step Two:
Pull the left strand around the back and through the loop you created.

Step Three:
Now cross the right strand over the left strand.

Step Four:
Pull the right strand around the back and through the new loop you just created, and tighten.

BOWLINE:

The bowline (BO-lin) creates a loop at the end of a rope that won't change size or slip. You can tie it around yourself—or another person—in a rescue situation.

Step One:
Create a loop in the left side of the rope (top over bottom).

Step Two:
Feed the right strand up through the loop.

Step Three:
Bring the right strand around the back of the left strand and feed it down into the loop. Tighten!

CLOVE HITCH:

The clove hitch is a quick, easy knot that can secure your line to a post, tree, or carabiner.

Step One:
Wrap the rope around an object, then bring the rope around a second time above the first wrap.

Step Two:
As you bring the rope around to the front, feed it through the loop you just created.

Step Three:
Tighten by pulling hard on the two strands, being sure to push the two loops together.

Out of rope? The string binding of this book can be removed in an emergency situation! (Keep the book's pages safe for reference—or to use as tinder!)

SHELTERS: FROM CAMPS TO CAVES

It may seem like finding food and water would be the most essential task for anyone in a survival situation, but the truth is that finding shelter is far more crucial. In fact, while humans can survive three weeks without food and three days without water, they won't last that long without shelter in inhospitable conditions. That's why finding or building a shelter should always be priority number one!

CHOOSING A CAMPSITE

Before you can consider pitching a tent or building a shelter, you'll need to locate a good site. There are a lot of factors to consider when searching for the perfect campsite, so be sure to take the following into account:

TEMPERATURE:

The higher the temperature outside, the more likely you'll want to set up camp at a lower altitude. But to get a little extra warmth when the temperature is low, set up camp on a sunny hillside or near a large exposed rock that will absorb heat.

WATER ACCESS:

Campsites should have easy access to water, but setting up right on the side of a riverbank or lake could make you more vulnerable to bites from the bugs that breed there, attacks by the animals that drink there, and rising water levels. Make sure water is nearby, but always keep a safe distance.

MOISTURE LEVEL:

No one wants a damp camp, as wetness rapidly reduces body heat. Make your camp on dry, level ground, avoiding areas that have poor drainage or could collect standing water.

VISIBILITY:

Making your camp near a trail or on the side of a hill will allow more visibility of your surroundings and might also allow anyone searching for you to locate you more easily.

POTENTIAL HAZARDS:

There are enough dangers out there already, so don't make it worse by choosing shelter in a high-risk area. Avoid steep slopes and any areas that might flood or threaten rock slides.

TRAIL TIP

Allow yourself plenty of time to find and set up your campsite. If you wait until it gets dark or you get tired, you'll have to settle for a less-than-ideal location.

TYPES OF
TENTS

Tents are portable forms of shelter that offer easy-to-assemble protection from the elements. There are dozens of types of tents out there, each with its own benefits.

RIDGE TENT:

This classic tent is probably the one that most people picture when they think about camping. Its simple triangular "A-Frame" shape is sufficient for protection but limits interior room thanks to the steep sides. Modified versions use curved poles to add more space and stability.

PYRAMID TENT:

Extremely lightweight and easy to carry, a pyramid tent consists of a single central pole that supports the tent. Pyramid tents aren't terribly roomy or sturdy, but they are a quick, easy option. If needed, a makeshift version can be created using a tarp and a long stick.

DOME TENT:

This popular tent uses curved poles that create an arched enclosure with plenty of headroom. It tends to be easy to transport and assemble. A dome tent is relatively versatile and resilient (except in high winds).

POP-UP TENT:

As its name suggests, this lightweight tent is designed to pop-up automatically when opened, with no assembly required. This makes it quite popular with inexperienced campers, but a pop-up tent is far less likely to withstand the elements.

TUNNEL TENT:

Using the same type of flexible poles as a dome tent, a tunnel tent uses a different orientation to increase room and maximize stability—as long as it is set up in the direction the wind is blowing and not against it!

PITCHING A TARP

It's okay if you don't have an elaborate store-bought tent that instantly assembles itself. With a tarp, some rope, and a few well-placed sticks, you can create your own tent in no time at all. Just follow these simple steps:

STEP ONE:

Tie a line of rope or wire between two trees. If you can't find two trees close enough together near your campsite of choice, find two sturdy branches and drive them into the ground to use as upright poles.

STEP TWO:

Drape the tarp over the line, so that the tarp is folded in half.

STEP THREE:

Tie shorter lines to each of the four corners of the tarp.

STEP FOUR:

Create stakes using small branches and tie them to the corner lines. Drive the stakes into the ground, stretching the tarp out to create an "A-Frame" shape.

ALTERNATE OPTION:

Instead of stakes, you can also weigh down the corners of your tarp with heavy rocks or logs.

DID YOU KNOW?

→ You can maximize your coverage and protection by suspending your shelter's center line closer to the ground.

→ There are dozens of other variations of tarp tents, including pyramids and tepees, so be creative and build the one that's best for you.

→ Tarps can also add an extra layer of waterproofing or groundcover to a store-bought tent.

SHELTERS 101:
LEAN-TO

Maybe you got stranded in the wild unexpectedly, without a tent or even a tarp. You can still make a decent shelter out of natural materials that will provide you a bit of extra warmth and protection from the elements.

A classic lean-to shelter is one of the quickest and easiest to build. It provides adequate protection from the wind and rain—as long as neither suddenly change directions.

STEP ONE:

Find a secure, solid surface—like a fallen tree or a large rock—to act as the spine of the structure. If you can't find a natural surface to use, wedge a sturdy branch between two trees.

STEP TWO:

Prop a row of long sticks against the spine at an angle, creating a solid wall that resembles one-half of a house's roof.

STEP THREE:

Cover the exterior of this one-sided structure with grass and leaves. If debris falls through cracks in the wall, add another layer of sticks to close the gaps.

TRAIL TIP

For extra protection, cover the open triangular sides of the lean-to with sticks as well. Just make sure you leave some room so you can get in and out!

SHELTERS 101:
DEBRIS HUT

The lean-to (see Pages 30-31) may be a quick, easy shelter under the right circumstances, but it requires the presence of a big, solid object to use as its primary support. When you don't have a large rock or a sturdy tree trunk to use as your anchor point, the debris hut makes for a fantastic freestanding shelter option.

A debris hut is a two-sided, wedge-shaped lean-to. It's slightly more complex to build, but provides additional protection.

STEP ONE:
Find a long "ridge pole" almost twice your height.

STEP TWO:
Prop up one end of the ridge pole using two short-but-sturdy Y-shaped sticks (or a low tree limb, if available), so that the top of the structure is at waist level.

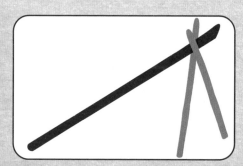

STEP THREE:
Line the two long sides of the ridge pole with shorter sticks to create walls.

STEP FOUR:
Cover those walls with grass, leaves, and other debris. Add extra sticks if the debris falls through the gaps.

STEP FIVE:
Slide into the open end and pull some extra debris behind you to cover the entryway and seal yourself inside.

TRAIL TIP

Don't make your shelter larger than necessary. The smaller the shelter, the better it will trap your body heat and the easier it will be to build. Make sure it's big enough for you to fit inside, though!

NATURAL
SHELTERS

Sometimes there's no need to build your own shelter at all. If you're really lucky, nature might provide one for you. In some regions with large rock formations and cliffs, indented areas at the base of the rock structure created by centuries of erosion are quite common. In many cases, these caves and overhangs can provide all the shelter you need.

SAFETY TIPS FOR NATURAL SHELTERS:

→ Before entering a cave or overhang, look for any signs of debris (such as fallen rocks) and check around the opening to make sure the stone surface is not flaking or crumbling.

→ Look for any signs of animals before entering—including tracks, hair, bones, or poop. If you think something might already have claimed this spot, it's safer to move on to another.

→ If you hear sounds of baby animals inside, leave immediately. An adult is likely nearby and could attack if they feel their young are being threatened.

→ Avoid caves that have wet floors in dry conditions, as they may be subject to flooding or heavy leaking during bad weather.

→ Be careful when lighting fires in a cave, as rapidly heating and cooling the rocks can create cracks that cause debris to fall. Plus, smoke alone is a potential hazard. It is safer to build your fire just outside the opening of the cave.

TRAIL TIP

Caves are commonly used as shelters by a wide variety of animals, including bears, wolves, cougars, snakes, scorpions, bats, and more. Even if there's no animal in the cave when you find it, one might come home later!

EXTREME SHELTERS:
COLD EDITION

Sometimes finding shelter isn't as easy as climbing into a cave or cobbling together a lean-to. When you're stranded in a less forgiving environment, such as a frozen wasteland, you might need to find a more creative way to protect yourself from the elements.

QUINZHEE: This snow cave is a variation of the igloo, but instead of being built out of icy blocks, the walls of the quinzhee [kwin ZEE] are constructed from tightly packed snow. Although the quinzhee is made of snow, your body heat in the confined space will keep you nice and warm.

To construct a quinzhee:

→ Mark off an area on the ground large enough that you can lie down comfortably, plus an additional two feet in every direction.

→ Break up the snow in the marked area with a shovel, turning it so that it is not heavily packed.

→ Shovel a large mound of powdery snow on top of the base area, creating a dome shape that stands about five feet (1.5 m) tall. Do not pack the snow.

→ Let the snow dome sit for at least an hour, allowing the snow to sinter (or harden). The longer you can wait, the better.

→ Insert a series of short, straight sticks in the exterior of the dome at multiple angles, about twelve inches (30 cm) deep. These will help regulate the wall thickness of the structure.

→ Start to tunnel into the quinzhee, creating the entrance on the downwind side. As you pull more snow out, you can crawl inside the mound.

→ Continue to hollow out the interior. When you reach the end of a stick, don't dig any further in that direction. Thin walls could cause the quinzhee to collapse.

→ Once your quinzhee is hollowed out to the proper wall thickness, remove some of the sticks to create air vents.

→ Get comfortable and keep warm!

TRAIL TIP

Since increased activity in the desert heat can quickly lead to dehydration and exhaustion, try to build your shelter in the early hours of the day, before temperatures reach their peak. And keep in mind that deserts turn extremely cold at night!

EXTREME SHELTERS:
HOT EDITION

When the desert sun is beating down on you, shelter is more important than ever. You might be able to find a cave or an overhang to provide adequate shade and protection, but if not, there may be another option—to dig! Creating a shelter below the ground can drastically reduce the temperature and could save you from succumbing to this unforgiving environment.

DESERT SHELTER:

All this shelter requires is a tarp (or a large piece of cloth) and a little bit of hard work.

→ Locate a low-lying area, preferably between two sand dunes, big enough for you to comfortably lie down. If you cannot find a proper depression in the sand, you may need to dig a hole, approximately 12 to 18 inches (30 to 45 cm) deep.

→ Use the excavated sand to create three walls around the edges of the hole, leaving one side open to use as an entrance.

→ Stretch your tarp over the top of the hole to create a roof, weighing down the edges with rocks or sand.

→ If you have enough fabric, fold the tarp over and create a second roof layer. Try to leave a gap of air between the two layers that is about 12 to 18 inches (30 to 45 cm). This space will help to substantially lower the heat level within the shelter.

OPEN DESERT SHELTER:

If you cannot dig, you can create a similar shelter using the same double-layered roof technique. In this version, all four sides of the shelter are open, and your tarp is raised above the ground using sticks or stacked rocks.

FIRE FACTS

Finding shelter may be the first step to surviving in the wild, but there's another key component that you won't last long without—fire! Once you know how to build a fire, a whole new world of possibilities suddenly opens up to you. Fire will help you keep warm, cook food, boil water, and even send distress signals in emergency scenarios. This section will show you how to heat things up while making sure they don't get too hot to handle.

FIRE SAFETY

Fire can do a lot of wonderful things to help you survive in the wild, but it can also become extremely dangerous if not handled with the utmost caution and respect. Before you even consider building a fire, it's important to know the following rules. They could very well mean the difference between keeping you nice and toasty or burning down the whole forest around you.

→ Your fire should be built a safe distance (about 10 to 15 feet— 3 to 4.5 m) from brush, trees, shrubs, and other flammable objects—including your tent!

→ Dig a pit (approximately one foot deep) and build your campfire in it to lessen the potential of unwanted spreading.

→ Clear any extra brush, grass, leaves, and even extra firewood from a ten-foot area surrounding your fire pit.

→ Fires should only be built on level ground protected from exposure to high gusts of wind.

→ Never build a fire in extremely dry conditions or in areas with an abundance of dead grass or foliage.

→ Look up! Make sure your fire isn't built under low-hanging branches that could catch fire.

→ If you're lighting the fire with a match, always discard the extinguished matchstick in the fire.

→ Your fire should be a size that you can manage. It's a lot easier to increase the size of a small fire than it is to reduce the size of a large one that is getting out of control.

→ Keep any flammable substances or combustible containers far away from the fire (at least five feet—1.5 m) at all times.

→ If it isn't something that is supposed to be burned (like firewood), don't burn it.

→ Always keep a bucket of water nearby to quickly douse flames that are spreading too fast.

→ Most importantly: Never leave a fire unattended!

GATHERING FIREWOOD

Before you can start a proper fire, you'll need something to burn. Luckily, the wilderness contains plenty of flammable options just waiting to be gathered, so you won't have to burn your map or your handbook yet! Here's a simple guide to what you'll need to collect in order to build the perfect campfire.

TINDER:

Tinder is the material you use to capture the first flames and keep them burning. Tinder can be more than just dead twigs. It can come in plenty of other forms, including dried grass, frayed rope, cotton balls, and even wads of toilet paper— unused only, please!

→ **Thickness:** The best tinder is around the width of a pencil tip, or slightly larger.

→ **Length:** Stretch out your hand and measure from the tip of your thumb to the tip of your pinkie finger.

→ **Amount:** Make a circle with both hands. Enough tinder to fill the space inside should do the trick.

KINDLING:

When the tinder has ignited, kindling is what turns it from a small flame into a full-fledged fire. Kindling wood is slightly larger than tinder and should consist of dead, dry twigs. Try to find branches that have already fallen off the tree, and avoid wet wood.

→ **Thickness:** No larger than the diameter of your thumb.

→ **Length:** From your elbow to the tips of your extended fingers.

→ **Amount:** Hold your arms in front of you and make a circle, then get a bunch of sticks that big.

FUEL:

Once the fire is burning strong, the fuel is what keeps it alive. When most people picture firewood, they're thinking of fuel: thick branches or even the split trunks of small trees.

→ **Thickness:** About as thick as your wrist. Anything thicker should be split, if possible.

→ **Length:** About the length of your whole arm, from shoulder to fingertips.

→ **Amount:** A substantial stack of wood, about knee-high from the ground, should be a good start.

This book's pages can double as tinder for a fire.

BUILDING A
FIRE

Now that you've collected the wood for your fire, you need to know what to do with it. Just throwing it all in a big pile and lighting a match won't do the trick. There's an art—or a science, really—to building the perfect fire in the wilderness. Here's what to do to make sure yours keeps burning strong:

TEPEE FIRE:

The easiest and most common type of campfire to build, the tepee fire is named for the cone-like shape created by the kindling and fuel.

→ First, take any tinder twigs and bend them in half, creating an up-side-down V shape. Put it on the ground and place any other tinder material—dried grass, leaves, paper, etc.—beneath it. Light the tinder with a match (or another method seen on Pages 50–51).

→ As the tinder begins to burn, start to place a few twigs around it in that familiar tepee shape, leaning against each other at the top for support. Start with just a few pieces of kindling and add more as the fire starts to catch, filling in the gaps as you go.

→ Finally, using the same process, start adding the fuel wood to create an even larger tepee. Add more fuel as needed and watch proudly as your fire rages to life, being extremely careful as you do!

TRAIL TIP

Surround the tepee's circular base with rocks after the fuel is in place. This will help to contain ash and embers and to retain some additional heat.

OTHER COMMON CAMPFIRES

The tepee fire may be the easiest type of campfire to build and master, but there are other options you can choose that might be worth considering, depending on your needs and your situation.

LOG CABIN:

Building a log cabin fire isn't that different from building an actual log cabin. Start with two pieces of kindling running parallel, about six inches (15 cm) apart. Next, stack two more parallel pieces on top running in the opposite direction, creating a square shape. Alternate a few layers back and forth until you have a solid structure. Add some tinder to the center, light it, then cover the top of the structure with small tinder twigs.

PLATFORM:

A wonderful fire for cooking and creating hot coals, the platform fire is similar in structure to the log cabin fire, but each alternating layer should have multiple pieces of wood placed side-by-side, creating a solid surface. The largest logs should be placed on the bottom, and the wood should gradually get smaller as you go up. Tinder is then lit on top of the structure and the fire burns down to the bottom.

STAR:

The star fire is a low-maintenance, long-burning fire great for situations where good fuel wood may not be abundant. Start a small tepee fire and surround it with three to five large logs arranged in a circular pattern with their ends pointing outward. As the logs burn down, push them in closer to the fire to keep it burning strong.

LEAN-TO:

Great for windy or rainy situations, the lean-to fire uses a natural barrier to protect your fire's early stages from the elements. Place your tinder on the ground directly beside a rock or a large green log, then place a layer of kindling over it at an angle, with one end on the ground and the other propped up by the barrier. Add a few more layers of kindling in the same slanted manner, followed by layers of fuel.

LIGHTING A FIRE

You may have built the best-looking pile of logs in history, but unless you know a way to get a fire started, it won't do you any good. Here are a few great options to get things burning:

MATCHES:

Perhaps the simplest method of fire starting, matches provide a flame with a single strike. Invest in waterproof matches if you can. They're not as cool as they sound (they don't let you light fire underwater), but they will be a huge help if you and your pack unexpectedly get caught in the rain.

FLINT AND STEEL:

This method is an old standard, where a piece of tempered high-carbon steel is struck against a piece of flint to generate an intensely hot spark. The spark only lasts for a fraction of a second, so be sure to keep it close to your tinder. Once the spark causes the tinder to smolder, blow on it until you get a flame.

Use the reflective page in this book to capture the sun's power to help light a fire.

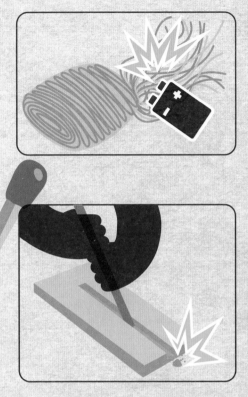

STEEL WOOL AND BATTERIES:

Steel wool is good for more than just scrubbing your pans at the end of a camping trip. Stretch out a six-inch (15 cm) length of super-fine wool and touch it with both the positive and negative leads on a battery. This should create a short but intense sparking glow across the wool. Avoid holding the wool itself, as it will get extremely hot!

FRICTION FIRE:

Friction creates heat, and heat can lead to fire. Sadly, lighting a fire isn't as simple as rubbing two sticks together, but you can create a fire plow by carving a rut into a two-foot-long (about 60 cm) piece of soft wood and quickly and repeatedly scraping a hardwood stick down that path. The resulting pile of wood dust should eventually combust—if your arms don't tire out first.

THE SUN:

The sun is a giant ball of fire in the sky, so why not use it to create a significantly smaller fire in your camp? Focus the power of the sun via convex lenses (like the ones in eyeglasses, binoculars, magnifying glasses, or cameras), aiming the resulting concentrated hotspot at your tinder. You can even polish the bottom of a soda can with a chocolate bar for an ultra-reflective surface that will create the same effect!

EXTINGUISHING A FIRE

Even if it looks like your fire is done burning, you can't just walk away from it without making sure that it is properly extinguished. Following these easy steps could prevent a few glowing embers from becoming a raging forest-sized inferno.

→ Extinguishing a fire can take a while. Give yourself at least a half an hour after the wood has burned down to ash to complete the process properly.

→ Once the wood has burned completely down to ash, douse the fire site with water until all embers are drowned and no hissing or crackling is heard.

→ Using a shovel, scrape embers off the surface of any remaining fuel logs, stirring them into the wet ash mixture. Douse with water again to make sure nothing has been left to smolder.

→ Add water until the entire fire site has cooled completely.

→ Rule of thumb: if it's still too hot to touch, it's too hot to leave.

TRAIL TIP

You may need a lot of water to drown your flames, so set up camp near a natural water source like a river or lake whenever possible. If you don't have an abundance of water available, follow the steps above using your shovel to stir dirt or sand into the embers, essentially burying the fire.

WHAT ABOUT WATER?

Now that you've built a shelter and started a fire, it's essential to start searching for the next key to survival in the wild: water. Staying hydrated means staying alive, especially in a survival situation. It doesn't matter if you're in a setting where fresh-water is abundant or one where even a single drop is a rare treasure. If you don't know how to find water or how to make it safe to use, you don't stand a chance of surviving for very long.

FINDING WATER

Clean drinking water is something we tend to take for granted. At home, a cool, refreshing drink comes as easily as turning on a faucet or opening a bottle. But in the wild, it might take a bit more work to find a suitable source of hydration.

→ When your mouth starts getting parched, trust your ears to help you find a nearby water source. Stand still to eliminate any noise you might be generating and listen for the sound of rushing water.

→ If there are no rivers, waterfalls, or streams around, follow these other signs to lead you in the right direction:

 → Groups of animal tracks that converge on well-worn paths may lead to watering holes.

 → Birds often circle over bodies of water.

 → An increase in the number of insects can be a sign of water nearby, as many species breed near wet areas.

→ If the local fauna aren't cluing you in, head downhill. Thanks to gravity, water naturally flows down into valleys and channels. The lower you get, the more likely you will be to find water.

→ If you can't find even a puddle, look for damp soil. It's worth digging to see if you can find an underground water source. Groundwater tends to be heavily polluted, but in a survival scenario, muddy water is better than no water.

→ Even if your water source seems clear and pristine, you should properly treat the water before drinking it.

TRAIL TIP

Stagnant water (like a lake or pond) has a much higher chance of developing algae, bacteria, and other potentially harmful contaminants than water that is in motion (like a stream or river).

PURIFICATION

Finding water is just the first step. Even if you've located a water source, there's no guarantee that the water itself is actually safe to drink. Untreated water can carry all sorts of deadly microbes and parasites that can actually *increase* your rate of dehydration if they make it into your system. To avoid consuming contaminated water, always purify your water using one of the following methods before drinking it.

FILTERS:

Portable water filters designed specifically for wilderness situations are widely available. These specialized pumps are capable of removing dirt and most harmful bacteria. Still, some waterborne viruses may be small enough to sneak through even the tiniest pores, so additional chemical treatment may be required if the water source is suspect.

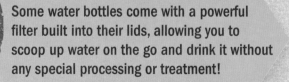

TRAIL TIP

Some water bottles come with a powerful filter built into their lids, allowing you to scoop up water on the go and drink it without any special processing or treatment!

TABLETS AND DROPS:

There are a number of commercially available purification tablets on the market, as well as chemical drops used to kill any diseases present in the water. These treatments use small doses of chemicals like chlorine or iodine, which can be dangerous to consume in large quantities, so be sure to read the instructions very carefully for the proper amounts to use. Chemical treatments often take a while to work before you can drink the water, and they can also make the water taste bad.

BOILING:

The most foolproof way to make sure that your water is free of any harmful biological contaminants is to boil it. Place water in a pot over your campfire and let it reach a rolling boil. Since recommended boiling times can vary depending on your altitude, it's best to play it safe and boil the water for a full ten minutes. It won't clean any dirt out of your water, nor will it be terribly refreshing until it cools down substantially, but it will certainly kill any bacteria or viruses lurking in the liquid.

ALTERNATIVE WATER SOURCES

Streams and ponds are great water sources when you can find them, but there are plenty of other ways to find water in nature. As with all water sources, it is always recommended that any water collected in nature be properly purified (using the methods discussed on Pages 58–59) before drinking.

RAINWATER:

Occasionally, bad weather can bring very good things. One of the fastest ways to gather water in the wild is to collect rainwater. Set out as many clean containers as you can during a storm to gather a large supply. You can even make temporary containers by stretching sheets of plastic into bowl-like shapes.

DEW:

The condensation that settles on leaves, blades of grass, and tree limbs in the early morning hours can be another great source of water. Tie some absorbent cloth (like a T-shirt, towel, or bandana) around your legs, walk through areas of tall grass, and then wring the collected dew into a container.

The foldable cup in this book can be used as a water collector container.

TRANSPIRATION:

Transpiration is the process in which plants naturally release water vapor into the air during photosynthesis. If you tie a plastic bag around a plant or a leafy limb of a tree, the vapor it releases will become trapped inside the bag and condense on its walls. The condensation will then run down to the lowest point in the bag, creating a small pool of water.

SNOW:

If you're in a snowy region, you're in luck, because the ground is already covered in frozen water. But be careful: snow and ice can be great sources of hydration—but only if you melt them first! Consuming them in their frozen state drastically lowers the body's temperature and can actually lead to dehydration and hypothermia.

SOLAR STILL

When fresh water is seemingly nowhere to be found, building a still might be the only answer to ensure adequate hydration. This simple two-part system uses the sun to draw the moisture out of your natural surroundings, distilling it into pure, drinkable water.

A makeshift solar still can be created using only two items—a clear plastic sheet and a small, clean container—plus a few rocks. Here's how to build it:

STEP ONE:

Dig a pit in an area that gets a lot of direct sunlight. The size of the pit is determined by the size of your plastic sheet. You should be able to completely cover the pit with the sheet. The larger your pit, the quicker you'll be able to collect a large volume of water.

STEP TWO:

Place the small container in the middle of the pit. This could be a bucket, a drinking glass, or anything that will be able to hold water.

STEP THREE:

Cover the pit with the plastic sheet. A great option is a plastic drop cloth used for groundcover in a tent, but you could even use a clear plastic rain poncho.

STEP FOUR:

Anchor the plastic sheet in place by putting rocks around the outer edges.

STEP FIVE:

Place a small rock in the center of the sheet, directly above the container, to weigh it down and create an inverted cone shape.

STEP SIX:

Let the sun do the rest. The heat passing through the plastic will evaporate any moisture below it, transforming it into vapor. That vapor rises, but gets trapped beneath the plastic. The vapor then condenses on the plastic, turning back into water droplets, which run down the slope of the weighted sheet and drip into the container below!

DID YOU KNOW?

→ Distilling water removes the majority of dirt, metals, pathogens, and pollutants, creating a very safe source of drinking water.

→ Under the right conditions, a good still can generate up to a quart of water in a 24-hour period.

→ You can use this same process to draw fresh water out of salt water! Instead of digging a pit, place the sheet above a large bowl of salt water with your empty container in the center.

PLANT LIFE: EAT AND AVOID

If you're out in the wild alone with nothing but plants to keep you company, you might as well put your new friends to good use. Forests and fields are teeming with plants that you can use to fill your stomach or to treat unexpected illnesses. But not everything green means go, so it's time to brush up on how to find the plants that help and to avoid the ones that hurt.

EDIBLE PLANTS

If you're stranded in the wilderness and you've eaten your last can of beans and your entire supply of protein bars, don't worry. Remember all those fruits and vegetables you eat every day? Well, they all come from plants. And while your favorites may not grow freely in the wild, it's likely that there are plenty of delicious alternatives sprouting up all around you.

BERRIES:

The forest is full of wild berries, but many of them can be extremely poisonous. It's best to stick with ones that you can easily identify, such as blackberries, raspberries, and strawberries. As a rule of thumb, steer clear of white and yellow berries, as only about 10 percent of those are edible. The darker the berry, the more likely it can be safely consumed.

DANDELIONS:

It's easy to recognize the bright yellow flowers of the dandelion—especially if you constantly battle to keep them off a perfectly mowed lawn. But these pesky weeds are completely edible from stem to flower and are packed full of vitamins. Their naturally bitter taste can be reduced if you boil them.

CLOVER:

You don't need to find a four-leafed version of this common plant to be lucky. A member of the pea family, clover can be eaten raw or cooked. It's another good source of vitamins, and the flowers make a nice tea. It's clear why honeybees love this common ground cover.

CATTAILS:

Typically found near the edges of swampy areas, the cattail is a versatile plant that has long been dubbed the "supermarket of the wild." Most of the plant is edible, but the lower white area of the stalk and the plant's roots tend to be favorites. Even the corn-dog-shaped flowers can be eaten, though you might want to save them and dry them out, as they make great tinder for your fire.

TRAIL TIP

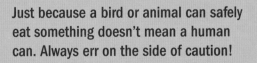

Just because a bird or animal can safely eat something doesn't mean a human can. Always err on the side of caution!

POISONOUS PLANTS

While nature's bounty is abundant, there are plenty of plants whose natural defenses make them extremely dangerous to anyone who consumes them. They may look delicious, but these poisonous plants might prove to be the last meal you ever order.

HEMLOCK:

A member of the wild carrot family, hemlock looks quite similar to its edible cousins. However, the toxins that reside in the plant's roots have earned it the designation of "the deadliest plant in North America." Two common varieties of hemlock, poison hemlock and water hemlock, can cause seizures and death when ingested—or even touched!

DEADLY NIGHTSHADE:

Although darker berries generally tend to be the safest, there's one pitch-black berry that may actually be the most toxic of all—the deadly nightshade. Ingesting even a few berries of the deadly nightshade, also known as belladonna, will lead to delirium, disorientation, and death. The berries aren't the only culprits, as the plant's leaves are poisonous as well.

RHUBARB:

Its celery-like stalks may make a great addition to desserts, but the leaves of the rhubarb plant are highly toxic. Consuming these leafy greens—whether raw or cooked—can lead to weakness, difficulty breathing, burning sensations, internal bleeding, and even death. Think about that the next time you order a slice of strawberry-rhubarb pie!

MUSHROOMS:

Much like berries, there are just as many poisonous mushrooms as there are safe ones. Unlike berries, however, the edible varieties are a lot more difficult to identify for an amateur forager. In general, it's probably best to steer clear of any fungus.

LEAVES OF THREE, BEWARE OF ME

While some plants are dangerous only if ingested, others can cause intense irritation simply by making contact with your skin. Encounters with poison ivy, poison oak, or poison sumac can all be avoided if you know what to be on the lookout for.

POISON IVY:

Location: United States and Canada

→ Leaves are pointed at the tip.

→ Leaves grow in groups of three.

→ Can be on a vine or growing as a shrub.

→ Usually green in the spring and reddish-orange in the fall.

→ White berries bloom in the spring and remain throughout the winter.

The simple rhyme "Leaves of three, beware of me" is a handy reminder to stay away from poison ivy and poison oak, with their clusters of three leaves, but they are far from the only plants growing that way.

POISON OAK:

Location: United States and Canada

➜ Leaf shape resembles an oak leaf.

➜ Leaves clustered in groups of three.

➜ Leaves are tooth-like in appearance.

➜ Leaves are fuzzy with hairs on both sides.

➜ Produces greenish-white or tan berries.

POISON SUMAC:

Location: Eastern United States and Canada, and southern United States

➜ Two parallel rows of six to twelve leaves with a single leaf at the tip.

➜ Individual leaves are oval or oblong shape with a point on the end.

➜ May have pale yellow or green flowers.

➜ May have yellow or white berries.

➜ Grows in swampy or boggy areas.

➜ Branches can grow up to 20 feet (6 m) high.

NATURE'S MEDICINE

Plants can be used as far more than just a good source of nutrition. Many wild plants and herbs can also help to cure common ailments. If you have developed any health concerns during your time in the wild, look around you for these natural remedies.

LAVENDER:

Although you might recognize its smell from your mom's favorite candle, lavender has been used throughout history to soothe all sorts of skin problems, including bug bites, rashes, and burns. Just crush the leaves and apply them to the affected area. Lavender also makes for a great natural bug repellent!

CATNIP:

It might not make you run around in a frenzy like it does for your favorite feline, but catnip does have a surprising effect on humans. A tea made from the leaves of the catnip plant has the ability to induce sweating, which is one way to reduce a fever.

YARROW:

Although its flowers look more like a big cluster of mini daisies, yarrow is part of the sunflower family. There's seemingly nothing yarrow can't do, but at the top of the list is wound healer: it can stop the bleeding of minor cuts and abrasions, and has the added benefit of being a pain reliever with antibacterial properties.

BUTTERFLY WEED:

Did you eat something that you're suddenly starting to regret? Follow it with a bit of butterfly weed to get it out of your system. The milky sap from the plant is an emetic [em ET ik], which means it stimulates vomiting. Sure, throwing up isn't fun, but it's way better than having a belly full of poisonous berries!

TRAIL TIP

A tea made from the leaves of blackberry plants can be used to ease stomach discomfort, including diarrhea.

ANIMAL ENCOUNTERS

You may be stranded out there in the wilderness, but don't worry—you're not as alone as you think. As far away as civilization may seem, the world beyond is teeming with life in the form of adorable woodland critters, majestic birds, and even dangerous predators. Remember, you're the stranger in their domain, so be sure to respect their home, or they may decide to bite back!

CRITTER-FREE CAMPSITES

Hear that scuttling sound in the brush? It's probably one of the many animals that make their home nearby your chosen campsite. They may be interested in you, but they're likely far more interested in all the delicious-smelling things you brought with you. Even the tiniest creatures can create havoc in camp, so take the following precautions.

→ Never feed the animals. If they know you've got delicious things, they'll assume you have more to share. Curious critters have no qualms about turning your camp upside down to find what they are looking for.

→ Store any food in a properly sealed container. There are even camping storage bins available that are designed specifically to eliminate food odors and prevent animals with crafty paws from opening them.

→ Hide surplus food safely out of sight. Once some animals identify a food container, they'll look for other similar containers and smash them open to get what they want.

→ Suspend your food from a tree. If it's in a sealed container, the animals probably won't notice it's there—but just to be safe, don't suspend it directly above your camp!

→ Don't use any scented lotions, soaps, or deodorants. To animals, all good smells are attractive, whether they come from food or not.

→ Keep a clean camp. Your garbage and food scraps are just as tantalizing to wild animals as your freshly cooked dinner. Seal all garbage in an odor-proof bag for proper disposal later.

→ For even better protection, cook your meals and clean your gear a safe distance (about 200 feet—60 m) from your camp.

FURRY AND FEROCIOUS

Some animals may seem like oversized versions of household pets like cats and dogs, but wild cougars, wolves, and coyotes are far from domesticated. If you come face-to-face with any of these common predators, you'll need to know what to do.

COUGARS:

Region: Western Canada and United States, Mexico, and South America

Identifying Features: Slender and agile; fourth-biggest cat species in the world; enlarged front paws with five retractable claws.

If a Cougar Attacks: Do not run. A cougar is likely to chase if you try to flee. Instead, face the cougar and maintain eye contact, as they prefer to attack their prey from behind. Try to make yourself look as big as possible. Children are more likely to suffer severe injuries during a cougar attack, so adults should pick children up or move directly in front of them.

WOLVES:

Region: Southern Canada, northern and western United States, and Mexico

Identifying Features: Broad face; large nose pad; short, rounded ears; large body; gray, black, or white coat.

If a Wolf Attacks: Wolves tend to hunt in packs, so if you run afoul of one, you can expect that more are on their way. Don't run, and don't make eye contact with a wolf, as that can be seen as a threat (or worse, a challenge). Instead, be big and loud and try to scare it away by shouting, waving your arms, and throwing things. As you do, back away slowly and make sure not to fall, as they will take advantage of any sign of weakness.

COYOTES:

Region: North America

Identifying Features: Narrow, pointed face; small nose pad; tall, pointed ears; smaller body than wolves; gray or reddish coat.

If a Coyote Attacks: Stand your ground. Make eye contact, loud noises, and big motions to try to frighten coyotes away. Banging pots, using an air horn, or blowing a whistle are all great methods of scaring coyotes. Due to their smaller size, coyotes are more likely to attack children and pets first, so always make sure they are protected.

BEAR NECESSITIES

Bears mostly want to be left alone, but they will attack if they perceive a threat to themselves, their cubs, or their food supply. The rules for a bear encounter vary depending on the situation, but there are some basic factors to keep in mind. Most importantly, it is key to understand the difference when you are facing down a brown bear versus a black bear.

GENERAL TIPS:

→ Travel in groups and speak at a comfortable volume to make your presence known.

→ Do not approach a bear to feed it or take a selfie.

→ Never get between a mother bear and her cubs.

→ If you cross paths with a bear, speak calmly so the bear knows you are not a prey animal. Stand still, but wave your arms slowly.

BROWN BEAR:

Region: Western Canada and Alaska

Identifying Features: Short and rounded ears; distinct shoulder hump; sunken facial features; claw marks are usually visible in tracks.

PLAY DEAD

If a Brown or Grizzly Bear Attacks: Lie facedown on the ground with your hands clasped behind your neck and play dead until the bear leaves. Keep your pack on if you have one and spread your legs so it's harder for the bear to turn you over. If the attack continues, fight back by focusing your blows on the bear's face.

BLACK BEAR:

Region: North America

Identifying Features: Tall and pointed ears; straight face; no shoulder hump; claw marks generally not visible in tracks.

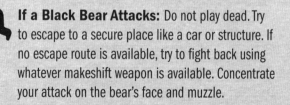

If a Black Bear Attacks: Do not play dead. Try to escape to a secure place like a car or structure. If no escape route is available, try to fight back using whatever makeshift weapon is available. Concentrate your attack on the bear's face and muzzle.

TRAIL TIP

Don't let the names fool you. Fur coloring on both brown and black bears comes in a range of shades from blond to black.

SINISTER
SERPENTS

If something on the ground is hissing or rattling, better take a quick step back! There's probably a snake nearby, and North America has a wide variety of highly venomous ones, including:

COTTONMOUTHS:

Also known as the water moccasin, the cottonmouth is a semi-aquatic viper found in the southeastern United States. The cottonmouth likes to hide in the water and attack suddenly, and its toxic venom can destroy tissue. If not treated quickly, amputation might become necessary.

COPPERHEADS:

Primarily located in the eastern United States, this close relative of the cottonmouth tends to "freeze" when people approach, rather than slithering away like most other snakes. That means it gets stepped on more, which means it's also more likely to bite. Luckily, the copperhead's first bite is usually a warning without any venom. If it feels the need to strike again, that's when the venom begins to flow.

RATTLESNAKES:

There is a wide variety of rattlesnakes throughout North America, including the diamondback and the sidewinder. All rattlesnakes share the same signature characteristic, a shaker at the end of their tail that creates a loud rattling noise to warn off potential predators. They're also highly venomous, so when they try to warn you, they really mean it!

DID YOU KNOW?

→ The rattlesnake's signature tail rattle is made up of multiple loose segments of keratin—a protein found in skin and hair—that click together when moved rapidly.

→ Every time a rattlesnake sheds its skin, its rattle gains a new segment.

→ The deadliest of all the North American rattlesnakes is the Eastern Diamondback, found in the southeastern United States.

WHEN SNAKES STRIKE!

If you're bitten by any snake in the wild, it won't be pleasant. If you're bitten by a venomous species, however, it could very well prove fatal if not treated properly and quickly. If you're exploring a region that is the natural habitat of venomous snakes, it's important to know how to keep clear of potential danger—and what to do if you can't!

AVOIDING SNAKEBITES:

Since you're probably not carrying a supply of antivenom with you, your best bet is to learn how to avoid bites at all costs. Here's how:

→ Stay on trails and avoid tall grass and underbrush.

→ Wear tall boots and long pants when hiking to create a strong bite barrier.

→ Don't ever touch a snake, no matter how awesome (or dead) it may look.

→ Inspect logs and rocks before picking them up, and look into holes or cracks before reaching into them.

→ Zip up your tent at night and check your boots before putting them on.

TREATING SNAKEBITES:

If you get a venomous snakebite, seek immediate medical attention, if possible. Before that:

→ Wash the wound with soap and water as soon as possible.

→ Keep the wound below heart level.

→ Take off any jewelry near the bite in case of swelling.

→ Wrap a tight bandage above the bite to slow circulation and the spread of venom.

DID YOU KNOW?

→ Alligators and crocodiles have existed for millions of years, surviving the extinction of the dinosaurs.

→ There are fourteen species of crocodile in the world, but only two species of alligator.

→ Crocodiles can withstand saltwater habitats, thanks to a salt gland that acts as a filter.

RISKY REPTILES

ALLIGATORS AND CROCODILES:

These giant reptiles have amazingly powerful jaws and are responsible for hundreds of deaths a year worldwide. Though they have some differences in their snout shape, tooth alignment, and preferred homes, alligators and crocodiles are frighteningly similar in their willingness to eat just about anything they find. While you should always use the utmost caution when near their habitats, if you find yourself staring down one of these scaly beasts, you still might be able to avoid becoming their next snack.

→ If a crocodile or alligator bites you and lets you go, it may just be warning you or defending its turf.

→ If it clamps down and tries to drag you underwater, its intent is to kill. Your only option is to fight back.

→ Try to stay on your feet, preventing it from dragging you too easily.

→ Don't bother trying to pry open its jaws, as they are some of the strongest on the planet.

→ Aim for its eyes and head, gouging and bludgeoning. If other people are around you, they should grab blunt objects and hit the creature in the head as well.

→ If the animal releases its grip, even just for a moment to readjust, use that moment to pull free and get to safety.

→ Seek immediate medical attention, as wounds can get easily infected by the high levels of bacteria in the animal's mouth.

INSECT INTRIGUE

Whether you thought it was comforting or mildly terrifying to learn that the wilderness is teeming with all sorts of furry and scaly critters, you'll definitely be shocked to learn how many more insects there are around you. It's estimated that there are ten quintillion insects alive on the planet! And while most of them are harmless to humans and beneficial to the ecosystem, there are some that should be avoided at all costs!

ATTACK OF THE ANTS

Ants can be found just about anywhere, from the dark depths of the forest to the cracks in the city sidewalk. Ants live and work together in large colonies, which they defend vigorously if threatened. While most species of ants are only an annoyance when they get into the house, some of them can be downright deadly!

FIRE ANTS:

A native species of South America, the red imported fire ant is working its way up through the United States, bringing its painful bite with it. They earned their name from the fact that their bite feels similar to being touched by a lit match, resulting in intense pain and red bumps that turn into white blisters. Fire ants will attack as a large swarm when provoked, latching on to their prey with their powerful mandibles and stinging repeatedly.

TRAIL TIP

Many ants, including fire ants, will often bite you even if you're wearing insect repellent. The best way to prevent bites is by being aware of your surroundings, staying away from anthills or any visible swarms of ants.

HARVESTER ANTS:

Found in the southern United States and Mexico, the Maricopa harvester ant is said to have the most toxic insect venom in the world, about twelve times stronger than a honeybee. The painful effects of its sting can be felt for hours. Even worse, it releases pheromones when it stings to summon other members of its colony to join in on the attack! It takes about 350 bites from harvester ants to kill an average-sized human.

PROTECT YOURSELF FROM PAINFUL BITES!

→ If a dangerous type of ant is crawling on you, brush it off before it bites. If you don't know if the ant is dangerous, play it safe and brush it off anyway!

→ If bitten, leave the area immediately, as there are likely more ants nearby.

→ If you come across an anthill, avoid the area. The less you provoke them, the less likely they are to attack.

→ Always wear long pants, socks, and boots when in the wilderness to reduce the ants' access to your skin.

STING
OPERATIONS

BEES AND WASPS:

Bees are fuzzy little insects that are very helpful, pollenating flowers and crops and making honey and wax. Wasps may look similar to bees, but they are far less helpful and far more aggressive. While bees do sting, most varieties only do so when threatened, and only once before they lose their stinger and die. Wasps, on the other hand, can use their stingers over and over.

BEE   **WASP**

AFRICANIZED HONEY BEE:

Region: Southwest United States and Mexico

Identifying Features: Smaller than normal honey bees; aggressive nature.

Africanized Honey Bee Facts: Also known as the "killer bee," this species is unusually aggressive for a bee. The slightest threat—from a loud noise to a wrong step—could send a swarm chasing after you for up to a quarter mile (400 m)! And once they're angry, they can stay angry for days. While the venom of the Africanized honey bee is not much more dangerous than any other bee's, it's the quantity of stings delivered by an attacking swarm that makes this species particularly dangerous.

IF BEES OR WASPS ATTACK:

→ Run! Don't stop until you reach a safe location that can be sealed off from the advancing swarm.

→ Swatting and waving your arms can draw attention and attract more attackers.

→ Use your shirt to cover your face, protecting your mouth, nose, and eyes.

→ If stung by bees, scrape off their stingers with your fingernail. Don't grab stingers to pull them out, as squeezing them may release more venom.

→ If you've been stung many times, seek medical attention.

ASIAN GIANT HORNET:

Region: Asia; some reports of them in the United States.

Identifying Features: Larger than normal wasps; quarter-inch-long (about 6 mm) stinger.

Asian Giant Hornet Facts: The world's largest species of wasp, the Asian giant hornet can grow to nearly two inches long (about 5 cm). Though it is not indigenous to the United States, there have been reports of it starting to make appearances in a number of regions in the U.S. While the Asian giant hornet is not normally aggressive, it will attack when it feels threatened. Its potent venom can kill an adult human with just a few stings.

WEB WARRIORS

While not technically insects (they're actually arachnids), spiders usually get lumped in with their creepy-crawly comrades. These web-spinning wonders can be a real benefit to the world around them, as they feed on many pests known to carry disease. Of course, it's hard to remember how helpful they can be when eight hairy legs start crawling up your arm! If just the thought of that creeps you out, you're not alone. The fear of spiders—known as arachnophobia—is one of the most common in the world. And with certain species of spiders, there's plenty of reason to be afraid!

BLACK WIDOW:

Region: North America

Identifying Features: Black body; red hourglass-shaped marking on enlarged abdomen.

Black Widow Facts: The black widow has earned its reputation as one of the most dangerous spiders on the planet. Not only does it kill its male counterpart after mating, its highly venomous bite contains neurotoxins that can lead to intense pain, nausea, cramping, convulsions, and even death for humans (especially children and the elderly).

BROWN RECLUSE:

Region: Central and southern United States

Identifying Features: Brown body; violin-shaped marking; six eyes.

Brown Recluse Facts: The bite of the brown recluse spider is a particularly nasty one, resulting in necrosis—the decaying of skin tissue. While you might not even feel their bite at first, intense pain will follow in a few hours and eventually lead to lesions and ulcers that can take months to heal and often leave permanent scars.

TARANTULA:

Region: Southern United States, Mexico, South America, and more

Identifying Features: Large body covered in hair; prominent fangs.

Tarantula Facts: Tarantulas seem more dangerous than they actually are, thanks to their gigantic, hairy bodies. Although they aren't nearly as deadly as the spiders mentioned above and will only attack if provoked, their enormous fangs can still deliver quite a bite that's as painful as a bee's sting.

DID YOU KNOW?

→ Other infamous arachnids include ticks, mites, and scorpions.

→ Scorpions have powerful pinchers on their front legs as well as tails capable of delivering a paralyzing sting.

→ The most dangerous scorpion in North America is the Arizona bark scorpion, found in the southwestern United States and northern Mexico.

APPALLING ARACHNIDS:
TICKS

Insects and arachnids may be small, but many species are natural carriers of deadly diseases. One bite from these tiny terrors may be all it takes to change your life for the worse, so be sure to bring your bug spray!

DEER TICKS:

Commonly found in wooded areas during warmer seasons, ticks are notorious for carrying a large number of disease-causing bacteria, viruses, and parasites. From Lyme disease to Rocky Mountain spotted fever, a tick bite on you or an animal companion can have long-lasting effects if not quickly and properly treated.

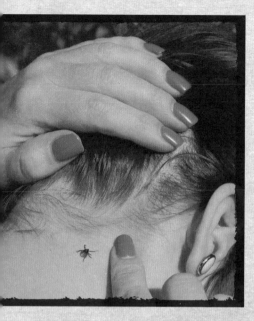

REMOVING A TICK:

→ Grasp the tick as close to the surface of your skin as possible, using tweezers. Avoid squeezing the tick, as it could release infected fluid into your body.

→ Pull the tick up and away in one steady motion. If you jerk or twist, the tick's head might pull off and remain embedded in your skin.

→ Once the tick is fully removed, clean the bite with rubbing alcohol or soap and water.

→ Keep the tick in a sealed jar full of rubbing alcohol or in an airtight bag, just in case it needs to be examined later.

→ If you develop a rash, pain, or any flu-like symptoms, seek medical attention.

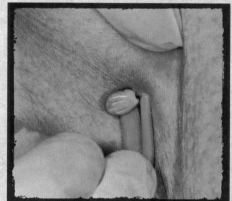

TRAIL TIP

Ticks tend to reside in wooded areas with tall grasses and shrubs. If you keep on a clear part of the trail and avoid brushing up against foliage, you're less likely to have one of these awful arachnids hitch a ride home on your skin.

INFECTIOUS INSECTS:
MOSQUITOES

MOSQUITOES:

These bothersome bloodsuckers are found just about everywhere, but especially near bodies of stagnant water, like ponds and marshlands. Mosquitoes have been known to carry and transmit a wide range of viruses, including West Nile and Zika, as well as severe illnesses like dengue fever and malaria. With so many potentially harmful results, mosquito bites should be actively avoided.

DID YOU KNOW?

→ The bumps and itching associated with a mosquito bite are caused by an allergic reaction to the insect's saliva.

→ Only female mosquitoes bite, as blood provides them protein they need for laying eggs.

→ A mosquito can drink up to three times its weight in blood in a single bite. Luckily, they don't weigh very much!

AVOIDING MOSQUITO BITES:

→ Mosquitoes are most active at dusk and dawn. Plan your activities, especially those near water, during other times of the day.

→ Wear light-colored clothing made of tightly woven fabrics. The less exposed skin, the better.

→ Use insect repellents as an extra layer of protection and be sure to reapply them frequently.

→ Mosquitoes aren't strong fliers, so even a light breeze may keep them away. A small fan can be a big help.

→ Insect netting can be the key to keeping mosquitoes off you while sleeping in an infested area.

→ Keep it cool. Mosquitoes prefer warm temperatures, and many species actually hibernate in temperatures below 50 degrees Fahrenheit (10° C).

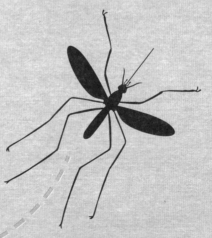

BUG BUFFET!

Hunger can make a person do desperate things, and if you're stuck in the wild without a source of food, being picky is no longer an option. When you need a quick burst of protein, there's nothing better than a crunchy, squishy, or gooey insect. Eating them may not thrill you, but (as long as you choose wisely) it certainly won't kill you either. In fact, when times get tough, bugs might just save your life!

GRUBS AND WORMS:

Easy to find in damp soil and rotting logs, grubs and worms both carry a lot of nutrients in their squishy, squirmy bodies. Slurping them down live might not seem like a terribly appetizing idea, so you might be better off cooking them first.

GRASSHOPPERS AND CRICKETS:

These common jumping insects are high in protein and easy to find—though not always easy to catch. They're less active in the early morning hours, so snatch them up for a crunchy breakfast. Always pull off their heads—which will also remove their guts—before roasting their bodies.

TRAIL TIP

Cooking insects before eating them reduces the risk of parasites or bacteria and also makes them a tiny bit tastier!

ANTS:

Not only are ants easy to find in just about any environment, they tend to travel in groups, which means a bigger meal for you. Collect a bunch and boil them to reduce the natural acids in their bodies. If you have to eat them raw, just make sure you kill them first so that they don't bite you back.

TERMITES:

Another high-protein option, termites are already a staple in many diets across the world. Colonies of termites can often be found devouring fallen logs. Since they keep themselves isolated from the world beyond, they tend to carry fewer parasites, but roast them anyway—it brings out their natural nutty flavor!

CREEPY CRAWLY CULINARY CAUTION:

While most bugs are safe to eat, it is best to avoid any insects that are:

→ Known to be poisonous

→ Brightly colored

→ Hairy or fuzzy

→ Foul-smelling

WILD WEATHER

It's hard enough trying to survive in the world under relatively normal circumstances, so what happens when the world decides to fight back? No matter where you go on the planet, there might be a natural disaster waiting right around the corner, ready to put your skills to the test. Whether you're fleeing from a forest fire or braving a blizzard, knowing what to do in each unique situation could drastically improve your forecast for surviving another day!

FOREST FIRE

You've already learned a lot about fire safety and properly extinguishing flames in the wilderness (Pages 41–53). Unfortunately, fire is a wild force of nature that doesn't like to be controlled, and under the right conditions it can spread to consume entire areas of forest at a rapid pace.

Forest fires burn up to 14,000 square miles (36,000 square km) of land each year in the United States alone. Traveling at speeds of up to 14 miles per hour (22.5 kph), they can change direction rapidly and will consume everything in their path—including trees, brush, and even homes.

THREE BASIC TYPES OF FOREST FIRES

GROUND FIRES:

These fires burn deep masses of dry, dead vegetation that is beneath the surface of the soil. Ground fires move slower than other types of wildfires, but can be far more difficult to extinguish.

SURFACE FIRES:

Burning mainly low-level debris, such as dry grass and fallen tree limbs, surface fires spread quicker than ground fires. However, they are also easier to suppress than other wildfires and tend to cause less lasting damage to the forest.

CROWN FIRES:

The most intense type of wildfire, a crown fire burns up the length of trees and then spreads across their tops. High winds can rapidly accelerate how fast crown fires spread.

FIGHTING FOREST FIRES:

Once a forest fire begins to rage, there's little chance you can stop it on your own. Leave it to the trained firefighting professionals to attempt to control the fire by depleting one of the three elements of the fire triangle—fuel, oxygen, and heat.

FUEL HEAT OXYGEN

If you are in the wilderness and encounter a forest fire, evacuate the area immediately. If a forest fire is approaching your home, make sure to clear any dry or dead vegetation from a 100-foot (30 m) radius to minimize the fire's ability to spread to the structure.

DID YOU KNOW?

→ Around 80 percent of wildfires are started by people, but they can also be ignited by lightning, downed power lines, hot winds, and even the sun!

→ Fire spreads faster moving uphill, so mountainous areas with steep, tree-covered slopes can be consumed quite rapidly.

→ Some wildfires can actually benefit the forest by clearing out overgrown vegetation, adding nutrients to the soil, and controlling pests and diseases.

IMPORTANT TIPS TO FOLLOW WHEN FACED WITH ONE OF NATURE'S DEADLIEST DISASTERS:

→ Stay out of moving water. It only takes six inches (15 cm) of water moving at six miles per hour (9.5 kph) to knock a person down and sweep them away—and only about a foot (30 cm) of moving water to wash away a car!

→ Keep to familiar ground. Even though some flooded areas may look calm and shallow, there's no telling when a sudden drop-off could change the depth from a few inches to a few feet. If you don't know the area, don't risk wading through it.

→ Choose your camp wisely. Rivers and streams can rise suddenly during periods of heavy or prolonged rainfall, so make sure your campsite is a safe distance from any body of water.

→ Move to higher ground. The lower you are, the more likely floodwaters could rush rapidly in your direction. When flooding is predicted, get to an elevated area fast.

FLOODING

Normally, when rain falls or snow melts, the water produced is absorbed by the ground or flows into rivers and streams to be carried away. When a large amount of water is produced over a short period of time, though, the ground can become oversaturated, and flooding can occur.

If the ground is exceptionally dry and the rainfall is unusually intense, it can cause a flash flood: a sudden, violent burst of extremely fast-moving water. Flash floods are the leading cause of weather-related death in the United States.

Flooding occurs all across the globe in all types of climates. If it can rain where you are, it can also flood. Flash flooding can even occur in areas that aren't currently getting rain. As the floodwaters build, they flow down natural pathways (such as dry riverbeds and hillsides) before eventually settling at the lowest point.

TRAIL TIP

Water isn't the only thing you have to worry about during floods. Flood waters can pick up damaging debris, displace dangerous animals, and carry a large number of infectious diseases.

BLIZZARDS

When the weather outside is frightful, it's usually time to come in from the cold. But if you're caught in a blizzard—an intense snowstorm with winds above 35 miles per hour (56 kph) and less than a quarter mile of visibility—you may find yourself stuck in one place due to a rapidly accumulating pile of precipitation. Hopefully, that place is warm and cozy—but if it's not, here are some hot tips for braving a wicked winter whiteout.

→ First, look for shelter. If there's not a man-made building nearby, you may have to build a makeshift shelter yourself.

→ Build a small fire to keep yourself warm and to fight off hypothermia and frostbite. Make sure to surround the fire with rocks to radiate extra heat.

→ Keep hydrated, but remember: Don't eat the snow! Always melt it first to avoid hypothermia and dehydration.

→ If you are stuck in a family car, stay inside the parked vehicle—but be sure to clear an area behind the tailpipe so that exhaust fumes don't pollute your air.

TRAIL TIP

If you're lucky enough to be indoors when a blizzard hits, stay there until the snow has passed. It's better to dig yourself out later than to find yourself without a way back in now!

DID YOU KNOW?

→ The snow that falls during a blizzard is only half the problem. The snow that's already on the ground can also get swept back into the air by high winds!

→ Blizzards can create whiteout conditions where intense winds and heavy snow mix together to reduce visibility to near zero.

→ The wind chill effect during a blizzard can make temperatures feel far colder than they actually are, increasing the speed at which frostbite and hypothermia (see Page 133) set in.

DID YOU KNOW?

→ Human bodies are three times denser than moving avalanche debris, which means they sink fast.

→ Avalanches are most likely to occur within 24 hours of a large snowfall (12 inches—30 cm—or more).

→ Avalanches aren't actually triggered by sound, so there's no need to cancel your yodeling practice.

AVALANCHES

Snow doesn't just fall—sometimes it slides. An avalanche occurs when large quantities of ice and snow rapidly descend down a steep slope, and it can be completely devastating to anything or anyone in its way. If you are unfortunate enough to be caught in an avalanche's path, you'll need to think fast!

→ If the ground starts to move, try to jump upslope first. If you accidentally caused the slide, you might have a chance to leap beyond its starting point to safety.

→ If the avalanche is coming from above you, move quickly toward the side of the slope. If you act fast, you may be able to get safely out of the way.

→ Drop your equipment. Heavy gear will just slow you down. It can be replaced—you can't!

→ Grab ahold of something sturdy. A tree or a big rock might anchor you in place until the danger passes.

→ If you get swept away by the rush of snow, try to swim with the current. Focus on keeping your head above the surface.

IF YOU START TO GET BURIED IN THE SNOW:

→ Keep one arm straight up towards the sky so you know which direction to dig to freedom.

→ Put the other hand over your mouth to capture air, then use it to dig an air pocket around your face.

LOST AND FOUND

The wilderness is a big place. Even if you think you're paying perfect attention, one wrong turn or misread map could send you spiraling off into the unknown. Understanding basic navigation skills may be the key factor in making sure that you don't get lost while in the wild, but when a map and a compass aren't enough to keep you on course, it's important to know what to do next to make it out of the woods safely.

NAVIGATION TOOLS

Some people have a natural sense of direction so strong that you can spin them in circles blindfolded and they'll still be able to point north. Most of us aren't that lucky. Fortunately, there are plenty of great tools—both high- and low-tech—to keep us going in the right direction.

MAPS:

In the olden days, long before there was an app for everything, maps actually used to be printed on big sheets of paper! They may not pinpoint your current location like a GPS system, but if you learn to read a topographical map, you can find everything you need to know about your surroundings—from the distance to nearby landmarks to your current elevation. And as a bonus feature, a printed map never loses its power.

COMPASSES:

The compass is a simple tool that tells you which direction you're headed. The needle reacts to the planet's magnetic poles, always pointing north. In combination with a map, a compass will help you get where you need to be a lot quicker than just crossing your fingers and hoping that you're heading in the right direction. And yes, there's a compass app on your phone, too, but why not save the power in case you need to make an emergency call?

GLOBAL POSITIONING SYSTEM (GPS):

These days, every smartphone seems to include an elaborate map of the world as a standard feature. Since most of the places you're likely to get lost probably don't have great cell reception, you might want to consider a handheld GPS. Not only do these dedicated mapping units link directly to a satellite network to track your location, they are also designed with more durable shells for rugged conditions and the option to change batteries when they run low.

TRAIL TIP

The "north" on your map and the "north" on your compass aren't always the same. In fact, they can vary as much as 20 degrees in certain parts of North America. If your map lists a "magnetic declination," be sure to adjust your compass to compensate.

CELESTIAL SIGNPOSTS

When you don't have a compass to point you due north, you can still get your bearings from the sun. No matter where you are, the sun always rises in the east and sets in the west. However, the sun isn't the only star that can help you find your way home. For centuries, travelers have used the night sky as a way to chart their course, whether on land or on the sea.

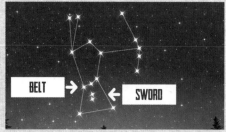

NORTH STAR:

Polaris is known as the North Star because its celestial location is in near-perfect alignment with the North Pole. This means that, as the Earth turns, Polaris seems to be the only star locked in place in the night sky (at least in the Northern Hemisphere). Polaris is a bright star located in the tail of the Little Dipper (Ursa Minor) constellation. The easiest way to locate it is to find the Big Dipper (Ursa Major) and follow a straight line up from the two stars on the outer edge of the dipper's cup. Those pointer stars will lead you right to Polaris— and Polaris will lead you north!

ORION:

Orion is a constellation that is easy to find and extremely helpful to use as a navigation tool. Orion's most distinguishing feature is its "belt," a straight line of three bright stars that run across the middle of its hourglass shape. The belt runs roughly east to west in the sky, but another line of stars that make up the "sword" that hangs below Orion's belt point to due south on the horizon. Orion may not be as readily visible in the Northern Hemisphere during the summer months due to the angle of the Earth on its axis.

ORION

FOLLOW
THE STARS

If you can't find a specific star in the sky to follow, the motion of any star can tell you which way you're going. As the Earth naturally rotates throughout the night, stars slowly seem to make their way across the sky. Noticing where they're going can help you get headed back in the right direction.

STEP ONE:

Put two sticks into the ground, approximately three feet (not quite 1 m) apart.

STEP TWO:

Pick a bright star in the sky and sit in a place where that bright star looks as if it is aligned with the top of both sticks.

STEP THREE:

Watch the star for about thirty minutes. As the Earth rotates, it will seem as though the star has moved. The direction it seemingly moves determines the direction you're facing.

→ You're facing north if the star shifts to the left.

→ You're facing south if the star shifts to the right.

→ You're facing east if the star shifts up above the top of the sticks.

→ You're facing west if the star shifts down below the top of the sticks.

TRAIL TIP

Stay in one place. If you get up, the chances that you'll return to the exact same vantage point are slim, so you might not get an accurate read on the star's motion. Thirty minutes may seem like a long time to sit still, but it's well worth the wait.

TIME TO S.T.O.P.

The sudden realization that you may be lost in the wilderness—or caught in the middle of any survival situation—can be quite frightening. When you first start to suspect that you may have gone astray, it's not time to panic. It's time to "S.T.O.P." Just remembering this simple word could make all the difference when it comes to getting back on track.

"S" IS FOR STOP:

If you remembered that you needed to S.T.O.P., then remembering what the first letter stands for is no problem. When you first realize that you may be lost, take a deep breath and get your bearings. Some people say that the "S" stands for SIT, as sitting down prevents you from continuing to wander as you fret about your predicament. Plus, it's easier to be found if you stay in one place.

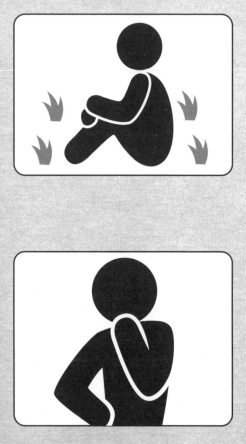

"T" IS FOR THINK:

Once you've stopped moving, it's time to think about how you got here. Where were you coming from? Which way did you go? Where could you have made a wrong turn? Were there any landmarks you passed along the way that could help your return? Those are the kinds of questions you need to ask yourself. You should also think about what kinds of resources you have on hand and how you will be able to use them if you're out in the wild for longer than expected.

"O" IS FOR OBSERVE:

Now that you've got a better idea of what happened, you need to get a better understanding of what's going on right now, including the terrain around you, the time of day, and the current weather. Taking the time to observe your surroundings is a crucial step to finding your way back. When you're scared, it's easy to lose focus of the small things around you. A simple solution to your dilemma may be closer than you think. During this time, it's important to observe your personal condition as well, making sure you haven't sustained any injuries and that you're feeling well enough to move to the next step.

"P" IS FOR PLAN:

Once you're fully aware of yourself and everything around you, it's time to forge a plan. This could include trying to retrace your steps using familiar landmarks, following the sound of nearby traffic to civilization, marching in a straight line towards the setting sun, or just staying put until someone finds you. Your plan should include realistic expectations about how long to wait before setting up camp for the night.

Reflective stickers, like the ones in this book, can be used to mark your campsite or a trail so you're less likely to get lost. Attach them to tree trunks or other solid surfaces.

SENDING
SIGNALS

So, your map is taking you in circles and you're sick and tired of being stuck out in the middle of nowhere? If you want to increase your chances of getting found, there are plenty of different ways that you can send signals to prospective rescuers. Not all of them are as easy as dialing a cell phone, but hey, if you could do that, you'd be home already!

WHISTLES:

There's no easier method to help you get found by someone nearby than keeping a small plastic whistle in your pack. Blowing three quick bursts on a whistle is the universal signal for someone in danger. Whistles are small and easy to lose, so get one that's brightly colored and has some sort of clip or ring attached. Sound only carries so far, so a whistle won't save you in every situation, but if you suspect that there's help nearby, it could assist them in determining your location.

TRAIL TIP

There are dozens of other ways to get your location noticed, including flashlights, glow sticks, flares, and giant letters made from strategically placed rocks. Be creative. Your life may depend on it!

FLAGS:

If you packed actual signal flags, they're probably already hanging by now. It's easy to forget how simple and effective a flag can be. All it takes is a stick and a large piece of fabric. Something brightly colored or reflective would work best, but even something white can be easy to see against the dark greens and browns of the wilderness. Hoist one above your location where potential searchers will be likely to see it, or wave it frantically if someone is passing in the distance.

MIRRORS:

A reflective surface is a great way to harness the power of the sun into a highly visible distress signal. A small signal mirror has the potential of shining a beam of light for miles, making your location a lot more noticeable to anyone who might be passing by. If you can see someone in the distance and they can't see you, aim that reflected light directly at them and move it around steadily until they can't help but notice that you're trying to get their attention!

The reflective page in this book works like a mirror for getting the attention you need!

SMOKE SIGNALS

If you made it this far in the book, then you already know how to build the perfect fire (Pages 46–49). If you've already got one raging, you might as well use it to help you get rescued. Sending smoke signals is an ancient but reliable method of delivering a message over long distances.

STEP ONE:

Get your fire burning strong. If the stress of the situation has caused you to blank on the basics, just flip back to the FIRE FACTS section (see Page 41) for all the important inferno info.

STEP TWO:

Although it's best to use only dead, dry wood as your tinder, kindling, and fuel, when the time comes to send smoke signals, you'll need something with a bit more life. Gather a bunch of fresh green branches and throw them on the fire to create an abundance of white smoke.

STEP THREE:

Soak a blanket or large piece of fabric in water, to prevent it from catching the flames. Once it's thoroughly wet, use it to completely cover your fire until no more smoke is escaping into the air.

STEP FOUR:

Quickly remove the blanket from the fire, and then immediately cover the fire again. This will send a huge puff of smoke billowing up into the air. Repeat this step as necessary to send the proper signal. One puff of smoke to show your location under normal circumstances, two puffs to show that all is well, or three puffs to call for help. No matter what, take extreme care during this step.

TRAIL TIP

If you don't have the ability to send smoke signals using your fire, you can still use steps one and two to create a signal fire with a large column of white smoke that is bound to draw attention to your location.

EMERGENCY!

No matter how much you know about survival, sometimes there's just no way to prevent things from going wrong. Accidents happen, and things can unexpectedly go from bad to worse in the blink of an eye. Even if you can't always stop tragedy from striking, being prepared to deal with the aftermath in the most effective way possible will give you a much better chance of turning things around.

FIRST AID KIT

No one should head off on an adventure without a first aid kit in their pack. When braving the wild, it's almost a guarantee that someone is bound to get an injury—whether it's just a minor scrape, a bad splinter, or something far more serious. No matter what the ailment, having the right treatment on hand can prevent infection and ease the pain until you can get things properly checked out.

FIRST AID KIT ITEMS:

BANDAGES:

The wilderness is full of unexpected ways to get injured, so having adhesive bandages in various shapes and sizes is a great way to protect small wounds. Also, be sure to include gauze pads, a gauze roll, and medical tape to wrap larger cuts, and moleskin to cushion blisters.

OINTMENTS:

A bandage might keep a wound clean, but it won't necessarily prevent infection. Applying an antiseptic cream will fight off any bacteria and aid in healing. Also, bring burn ointment to help ease pain from prolonged sun exposure and minor fire-related mishaps.

Seal any medicines and ointments that are strong-smelling or prone to leakage in a plastic bag within your first aid kit. Remember, if it smells good, critters don't care if it's food or not!

MEDICATIONS:

Every first aid kit should include basic medications, including pain relievers (such as aspirin) and antihistamines. Personal medications should be packed as needed. These can include daily vitamins, prescription medications, and even EpiPens for those with severe allergies.

TOOLS:

Although most of your essential tools were already included in your pack, you may need a few extras for your first aid kit. Tweezers help to remove splinters and ticks. Scissors help to cut bandages (and string for your tent). A magnifying glass can help you find small debris in a wound. Even nail clippers and a needle and thread come in handy more often than you'd expect.

STERILIZATION:

If you're using tools for medical reasons, it's important to make sure that they are clean. Washing them with rubbing alcohol or hydrogen peroxide first will make sure that they are sterile and ready to use.

TREATING BURNS

Hopefully, the only burn you'll get during your time braving the wild is the burning desire to go on another adventure. When you're building fires, boiling water, and cooking food, though, there are plenty of chances for something to go wrong. Maybe your campfire unexpectedly spread out of control or you accidentally grabbed the hot handle of your pan. Whatever the cause, if you get a serious burn, you need to know how to treat it properly.

STEP ONE:

Eliminate the source of the burn. If you grab something, like a metal pan, that's too hot to handle, just drop it. If fire has spread to your clothing, fall to the ground and roll around until the flames are extinguished. Remove any clothes or jewelry that may still be smoldering and retaining heat.

STEP TWO:

Expose the burn site to cool water for several minutes. Pour water over the affected area or apply damp cloths to the burn. Avoid ice-cold water, as it can constrict blood vessels and cut off oxygen and nutrients to the burn area.

STEP THREE:

Assess the severity of the burn to determine how bad it is and how much of your body it covers. There are three types of burns:

→ **First-degree burns**: Though painful and red, these superficial burns only affect the outer layer of skin and don't include blisters.

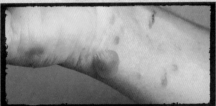

→ **Second-degree burns**: Deeper burns that go below the surface of skin, they appear red, wet, and blistered, and they take longer to heal.

→ **Third-degree burns**: These burn through your skin's layers and into the tissue beneath. The burnt area looks leathery, charred, often gray or white, and sunken; however, these burns aren't painful because nerve endings have been completely scorched away.

STEP FOUR:

If you have any third-degree burns, second-degree burns around your face, hands, or feet, or burns on more than 10 percent of your body, you should seek immediate medical attention. If your burns are minor, you can treat them on site as follows:

→ Wash the burn area thoroughly with clean water and soap.

→ Apply an antibiotic ointment to the burn.

→ Dress the wound with clean gauze.

→ Change the bandage once or twice a day, regularly checking for signs of your injury getting worse instead of better.

ANTIBIOTIC OINTMENT

HEATSTROKE

Extreme temperatures can have powerful negative effects on the human body. It doesn't matter whether you're too hot or too cold; either way, the effects could be devastating if not caught early and treated properly.

Heatstroke, also known as hyperthermia, is a condition that occurs when the body's core temperature goes higher than 104 degrees Fahrenheit (40° C). It results from long periods of exposure to or increased physical activity in very hot environments. Symptoms of heatstroke include severe headache, physical weakness, light-headedness, shallow breathing, and hot, red, dry skin. These symptoms are accompanied by a noticeable lack of sweat, due to dehydration.

If you suspect that a companion might be suffering from heatstroke, it is important to call for medical assistance immediately. Once help is on the way, try the following to reduce the person's body temperature and prevent the condition from worsening:

→ Get them to a shady area and remove any heavy clothing they may be wearing.

→ Wet their skin with cool water from a damp towel or sponge.

→ Submerge their body in cool water, such as a lake, stream, or tub. Be sure to support their head above water in case they are too weak to do so themselves.

→ If ice is available, apply it to areas of the body with a high concentration of blood vessels (such as the neck, back, groin, and armpits).

HYPOTHERMIA

The opposite of hyperthermia is hypothermia, a condition where the body's core temperature drops below 82 degrees Fahrenheit (28° C). As you probably guessed, hypothermia is caused by extended exposure to extremely low temperatures without proper protection. Hypothermia's symptoms include shallow breathing, weak pulse, disorientation, drowsiness, and intense shivering. Hypothermia can also cause confusion, which can prevent the victim from realizing the very real danger they are in.

As with heatstroke, immediate medical attention is recommended for anyone suffering hypothermia. Before help arrives, attempt to gradually warm up their body using these methods:

→ Get them indoors or to an area that is protected from the cold and remove any wet clothing they may be wearing.

→ Dry their skin and wrap them in blankets, towels, or dry clothing. Focus on warming their torso and head first.

→ Don't submerge them in warm water, as warming the body too quickly can cause other health problems.

→ If hot-water bottles or heating pads are available, wrap them in towels and apply them to the neck, chest, and groin.

BROKEN LIMBS

Accidents happen, even in the most controlled situations. In an unpredictable outdoor setting, the number of potential dangers that could lead to serious injury greatly increases. Nature trails don't come with safety rails, and misjudging one step on a steep path could lead to a fall that breaks more than just your confidence.

If you find yourself with a broken limb in the wild, here's what to do:

SET IT:

In most cases, you'll want to move a broken limb as little as possible to avoid doing any further damage. But in some more severe breaks, you might need to "set" the bone back in its proper position. Returning the bone to its natural alignment will help to reduce pain and prepare the limb for immobilization.

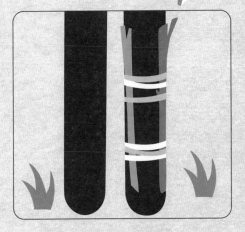

SPLINT IT:

Once the bone is oriented correctly, you'll need to prevent any further motion of the injured area. To achieve this, create a splint by using two sticks (as long as the limb and about one to two inches—2.5 to 5 cm—in diameter) placed on opposite sides of the limb. Secure the sticks in place with rope or pieces of cloth at the top and bottom of the limb, preventing it from moving or bending.

TREAT IT:

The best way to make sure a broken limb heals properly is to get to a hospital for immediate medical attention. While moving someone with a broken leg may require professional medical assistance, a person with a broken arm will likely be able to make it back to civilization safely on their own (though they may require a bit of extra help).

TRAIL TIP

Severe injuries can sometimes cause a person to go into a state of shock. If a companion with a broken limb suffers from an elevated heart rate, nausea, dizziness, chills, or starts to look pale, it's time to take a break and call for help. Keep them warm and hydrated (and off a broken leg) until assistance arrives.

DROWNING

When bodies of water are involved, drowning is always a danger. Even the best swimmer can suddenly succumb to fatigue or the pull of strong undercurrents. If you see a companion struggling to stay afloat, you may have to use one of the following options to get them back safely to solid ground.

REACH:

This method works if the person drowning is relatively close to the shore. Make sure you are in a secure position where you cannot be pulled into the water. Lie flat on the ground and reach out toward the victim with your arms. If you can't reach them yourself, extend a sturdy branch or pole and pull them to safety.

THROW:

If you have a flotation device on hand—like a life jacket, an inflatable cushion, or even a beach ball—throw it out to the victim so that they can hold on to it and stay above water. If possible, you should tie a rope around the item and pull them back along with it.

ROW:

If you can't reach the victim or throw them a flotation device, you might be able to get in a boat (or kayak or raft) and paddle out to the victim. Once there, give them a flotation device before using the Reach method to get them safely to the side of the boat. Be careful that they do not tip the boat and pull you in along with them!

GO:

If the victim is too far out in the water and a boat is not an option, you may have to swim to help them. However, it is not recommended to attempt a swimming rescue unless you are both a strong swimmer and you have a flotation device. Drowning victims are desperate to stay afloat and will instinctively push you under in an attempt to save themselves. Once you reach the victim, use your float for support and swim on your back towards the shore, towing the victim with their face up and their back to you.

DID YOU KNOW?

→ A drowning adult might be able to stay above water for three minutes, but a child might last less than 30 seconds.

→ Drowning can occur anywhere, from the ocean to a swimming pool to a bathtub. A large body of water is not required.

→ It is estimated that almost 85 percent of drownings could be prevented with proper supervision, equipment, and swim training.

PERFORMING CPR

If someone has stopped breathing, you may need to try to revive them using CPR, which stands for cardiopulmonary resuscitation. CPR is a basic skill that everyone should know, and there are courses available to become trained and certified in it. CPR could save a life in any number of everyday circumstances—from drownings to heart attacks.

STEP ONE:

Once you've determined that the victim is not breathing or responding, immediately call for medical assistance (if possible) before beginning to perform CPR.

STEP TWO:

Overlap your hands in the middle of the victim's chest and use your body weight to push down about two inches (5 cm). Repeat this at a rate of about two compressions (pushes) a second.

STEP THREE:

If you have CPR training, complete 30 compressions, and then gently tilt the victim's head back with one hand while lowering their chin with the other to open their airway. Check for any signs of breathing for five to ten seconds. NOTE: If you are not trained in CPR, continue with the "hands only" method described in Steps One and Two for 100 compressions before checking the victim's airway.

STEP FOUR:

If trained in CPR, move on to mouth-to-mouth breathing. Hold the victim's nose shut and make a seal around their mouth with your own. Blow a strong breath into their mouth for one second, followed by another. If their chest does not rise after the first breath, open their airway again (as described in Step Three) in case there is an obstruction.

STEP FIVE:

Following the two rescue breaths, begin the cycle over again—performing 30 chest compressions, checking the airway, and administering two rescue breaths—and repeat a total of five times. NOTE: If you are performing the "hands only" method, repeat five cycles of 100 chest compressions, checking the victim's airway between cycles.

STEP SIX:

If the victim is not breathing by the end of the fifth cycle, they may require other methods of resuscitation, such as a defibrillator. If you or someone else called for help, keep performing CPR until a professional arrives to offer assistance.

CONGRATULATIONS!

You survived until the end of the book and gained a lot of valuable knowledge along the way!

But knowing what to do in emergency situations is only the first step. Actually being able to apply the information you learned when those scenarios arise is a slightly different story. The best way to make sure you'll be able to use these techniques when things get rough is to practice them in advance under more controlled conditions.

That doesn't mean starting random campfires in the backyard or building debris huts in your living room, of course, but it does mean taking a deeper look at the world around you everywhere you go and thinking about how the information discussed in these pages might apply if something bad were to happen without warning.

Hopefully, you're never in a circumstance where you need to use the skills described in this book—but if you are, then understanding the right things to do and how to do them can be more valuable than any tool you put in your pack.

Survival still won't be easy—but if you empower yourself to face these challenges head on, it will most certainly be achievable!